afloat

a raft of water poems

sheryl massaro

ISBN: 979-8-9887537-1-1 (Paperback)

LCCN: 2023920357

Front cover image by Sheryl Massaro
Book design by Sheryl Massaro
Font used throughout is Helvetica

Printed by DiggyPOD, Inc., in Tecumseh, MI, USA

First printing edition 2023

Sheryl Massaro
FAC Artist Studios
7 North Market St., Suite 25
Frederick MD 21701
www.sherylmassaro.com

on our kinship with water

with thanks to

The Louisville Review, Spring 2021,
for publishing *The Water Tasting* and
Precipitation

Honeyguide Literary Magazine, October 2020
for publishing *Rain Forest*

Passager Press 2019 Competition
for publishing *What We Are*

contents

from a distance

in the watershed

the surf

the spa

images — from oil paintings by sheryl massaro

from a distance

Broken Water, Sheryl Massaro ©

how water came to earth

no lights on this table,
just sporadic, burning stars
from the tips of cigarettes.

a player feels for the rack,
lifts it slowly, has no clue
where to put it, in the dark.

he drops it toward the floor
where it never lands, but
a crack from his cue

finds the key ball,
breaks the triangle,
a shape older than thought

and there, in the darkness,
orbs scatter like flat fireworks,
some to black holes,

some to the bumpers,
many wavering in the expanse.
it is the felt that slows them,

its nap a gravity muffling
their momentum, though some
barrel into each other

with such force
their polished skins
chip, embed
in the rind of another.

a body of waters

faster than light years
come the empty vistas
and winds of mars.
at once familiar and strange,
the reddish terrain
of rubble disappoints
in the sunlight
from our common star.
my substantial stone
of an imagination plops
into the crater that might
have rippled with water
in a distant, distant past.
and with moisture
might have come life,
but i doubt the kind
that could be stunned
by the stars in a martian
night, could muse on
how different they appear
from another planet.
i imagine what our blue
earth must look like
from such a distance,
our very busy, very
beautiful, wet,
rippling home.

walking on water

on the planet of miracles
there are the moving waters
and the still waters,
the salted and fresh
and the brackish,
warm and frigid,
shallow and deep.
we bring them vacations,
offerings of inflatables
and motors and paddles
and skis, skates, and augurs
drilling ice for fruits of the seas.
on the planet of waters
we drink and bathe
and baptize and drown
and float and boat
and burn our hands
in geysers, on ice.
we are puddles in skin,
wet brains, weeping eyes,
sweat. everyday, everywhere.

evolution

in the waters
is where most life lives
and the boy imagined
being huddled
on a spit of land,
with others in the pack
of 1 out of 10 creatures
that do not live wet.

he waved his hand
through the air
and thought of
how sluggish
the same wave
would feel in water,
and yet his body
would be borne
like a duck
or a duck's feather
to wherever
or maybe whenever.

why come ashore?
as strange as trying life
in the sky with no wings,
so many fatal tumbles
before body cells
spark with evolution.
from water to land
after food, curiosity,
a sweetheart, peace.
water to land, muffled
to din, tides to wind,

yet sometimes back again
as if through a portal
seen only by those
who wander the worlds.
some who, like mermaids,
choose to dwell in many.

what we are

jostling down the street
picking up bits of you
and you and leaving me,
all just gravitating,
obliviously giving
as we pass and rub, taking.
viruses, dna, stories,
problems, sweat,
like h_2o deposited
from an asteroid
as it bumps a planet,
or like finding water
snug as a sweet ovum
embedded right here
in our own stone.

omens come

the omens come,
infinitesimal,
older than earth,
and off we go
for comfort
to the waters
that will talk with us,
the ungainly bodies
rocking in lake beds,
slipping downstream,
spinning down a drain,
heaving against gravity
to reach our shores.
a liquid language
of soft chatters,
wet clucks,
basso crashings,
close whooshings
trailing off to echoes
in the endless pipes
going, going.

hard water

we live in cold pearls,
an arc of ice houses,
not for but made of,
domed and lustrous
in the morning gold.

we wait. food and furs are coming,
dogs and men. they ride in mirages
on the horizons. bear, fox, seal,
the tang of seared meat, smoky fish
we gnaw in our dreams.

a lullaby drifts among us,
a soft vibration from mothers' mouths
to children's spines, untying their tensions.
clean stomachs moan through the pale nights.

to build a house on sand,
to build a house on rock.
to build on things that thaw,
tundra and ice.
foundations that break and move
and take us with them.

the canoe in the trees

you might have sailed
an ancient flood
to find your first home
high among the trees.

you might have yearned
to be a mighty trunk
again, riding the wild
currents of air.

when i climb to reach you
in your crook of a bough,
will i find the skeleton
of an antediluvian,
or will your hull
be empty, open
to any fiction?

you might agree
to return with me
to the rivers, or i might
shimmy down alone
as you stay aloft,
paddles folded,
gathering snow.

the sunken continents

no one knows for sure
just how many continents
have drowned. zealandia
of the south pacific, mauritia
off africa, the kerguelen plateau
in the vast indian ocean.
those are just the actuals.
then we have mu, lemuria,
atlantis, terra incognita,
imagined worlds under swaths
of open water. invariably,
their mythic civilizations
were beautiful, brilliant,
still speaking words of insight
even now to ordinary people
who believe they are
descendants. maybe.
or maybe the sunken lands
themselves have formed us.
we might all be
the very special children
of earth and atmosphere,
and that would be
incredible enough.

a blue

below the tip,
there is nothing
but fathoms of time
held fast in stillness
like flies in amber.
whales rub away
their itches on its flanks.
bears lumber,
cubs roll, seals bark
in breathless coldness.
we see it as a blue,
impossibly far off
cubist image, inert,
eternal, impregnable
to a softer things
such as warmth.

rohrshach

there is an angel in
an algae-laden pond,
shimmering in heat
and dappled acid light.
an angel canoed
in its wings, afloat
in mute ecstasy
at the touch
of this earthly
liquid, water.

feather by feather
the furled wings
drift apart enough
to bare two beings,
heads bent, sky eyes
touching, tingling,
in love in this
different heaven.

in the watershed

River Runs through It, Sheryl Massaro ©

crossing the bridge

through the golden battlefields,
paralleling a railroad track,
the river moves on to the potomac,
an old native name, and i wonder
if those first ones saw this fluid
splashing through its bed,
the sky rafting on its surface,
and felt the lift inside as i do,
a brief, unforgettable levitation
as sight rests on light resting
on the belly of this otherwise
strangely colored, confident river,
the green-grey of silt formed
from the settling paint
of an artist's soaking brushes,
a color always murky
and never the same.

the watershed

green tentatively spreads
partway up the mountain
as snowmelt, at first,
picks its way down
and ends in a tumble.
water seeking its level,
its sweet spot.
thirsts are slaked,
fields watered, fish caught,
kayaks launched.
to the hawk above,
everything flows everywhere
in rills and creeks, brooklets,
streaming from the mountain
shoulders across the lowlands
where we gleam and quiver
like dew on a web.

the skeleton flower

the shaded mountains of asia
and appalachia shelter her,
a pearly blossom, little sister
to the rhododendron, flushed
and pendant, the camellia,
wisteria, iris. young women growing
fertile on the hillsides. already they
have much to bear without
the weight of afternoons rains,
but the little white petals
of the skeleton flower
become the rain,
turning perfectly clear,
cupped, invisible.

ghosts

we all should go home in mango season,
at the end of the monsoons,
when the sweet reddening paisleys
dangle like sexual somethings
and the bark is as dark and glistening
as braids and the feet of everyone
are equally wet.

but we go home in an indian autumn,
when the dry sky is too blue to be
believed, home to whitening parents
who see the lines in our skin as well.
we lounge on verandas of the now
public mansions, leaving the salons
behind us to the long dead
whose beautiful perfume we sense,
and a faint ring of bangles,
as if a great party goes on.

rain forest

at dawn
and through the day
the wattled bellbird
gongs as if appointing
the moments for
faunal instinct,
floral bloom.

one by one,
the coevolution
of leaf and caterpillar,
flower and hummingbird,
herbivore, carnivore,
and omnivore resumes,
while all existence
drinks or drips.

sunset comes early
to the wet mountain
and ebbs in the long blue
shadows of quetzal tails
and dangling sloths,
in the quiet devolution
of day into dark
where the translucent
night-frog harbors
its conspicuous heart.

flash drought

the truth of the term is in question,
yet all understand crops turn brittle
when rains, then roots fail.
there's life, and then death,
like life before a crash
and right after.

there are photos of this farm,
that lawn, those rose beds,
these pumpkins, microscopic cells
of the planetary land mass.
Images from miles up, a safe
distance from the tumult of weather
and the dread of repetition.
another dust bowl? we wonder
as years grow drier.

a region on brazil's coast
has dunes so vast
they become a desert.
but with the rains,
lagoons bloom between
the sandy hillocks.
green things sprout,
even fish appear.
from above, the lagoons
look like scattered jewels,
yet grow clouded
by the earth's next orbit
and are figments
in the one after that.

rio amazonas

the frozen mouth thaws,
and small splashes
of river begin the search
for their thousand homes
just below the equator.
they nurse on the blackwater
mothers, and the whitewaters,
and the one clearwater.
they never starve,
they never stop merging
and splitting a continent.

from a distance,
there is a constant cloud
above the tree canopy.
vapor from the clear mother
who sleeps on hot rock
and boils in pools
and waterfalls,
who offers her heat
to the massive river.

it pauses in its rushing,
breaks a sweat, but
there is a horizon to find,
an ocean of salt to die into.

water falling

come with me, let's see
what all this falling is about,
what the water carries
over the edge.

the terror of a limb
lightninged from its trunk,
a bear cub caught and spun
in the rapids, a raft of tourists
dreading descent.

there comes a moment
when the water loses breath,
and its clamoring passengers
rest in the sky, weightless.

below the water, there is land

it rained for 960 hours,
40 days and nights,
and there was no place
for that water to go
except on top of this,
on top of that,
and its bulk grew
like swelling fat cells
sloshing here, there,
everywhere until it was
tired, tired of growing
and it began to sleep,
and as it slept, it settled
and soaked into all
it had fallen on.
it had strewn boulders,
filled canyons, drowned
the prehistoric caves,
bathed the deserts,
snuffed volcanoes, filled
what had been skies.

but now, rest.
now, the water's surface
has sunk like cheeks
of the dead. the land breathes
above the oceans again
and, from beneath,
holds them afloat.

snow

strange visitors,
these crystals,
dropping softly,
determined to cast
monotoned, muffled
neutrality to land
and time.

we pause
when snow comes,
look, go outside
to see, feel, wonder
if this beauty
will be too much,
if these feathers
will gel and freeze
and break things.

and what of snow
will we remember
when the bees buzz
and toes nuzzle grass
and ice clinks in glasses
we press against
our sweaty foreheads?

tundra

picture siberia sagging,
melting like a witch
at the touch of water,
belching methane,
ceding its vastness
to puddles and tusks
of mastodons.

this ground. it takes
our dead and waste,
bears the weight
of pavement, homes,
bodies, gives us beds
on its grasses,
buries us in peace
as long as it is dry.

the quiet season

at the edge of the pueblo,
someone always has listened
to this water. anyone fleeing a spat
or yet another sharp blue sky
or the darkness inside
or tourists
or dust.

dogs have drunk it,
then scuffled on the banks
for territory. it has rinsed skin
and clothing and blood.
it has sent yellowed leaves
and urine on their ways,
has shown the sun and moon
their faces and us ours.

this water
has never taken a breath
in its conversation,
even in the quiet season.
even when its own skin hardens
in the cold, it erodes
from the gurgle beneath.

atmospheric river

she sensed a river
coming overhead,
settling into place
like a massive dread
a mile deep, a thousand long,
full of the damp skies
from here to the other side
of the pacific.
it was like the ancient
biblical tale of realms
of waters on earth
and also above.
she imagined it laden
with strange, ephemeral
creatures, peculiar flora
on its banks, all destined
for death as the river dropped
its load at landfall.
but i'm mistaken, she thought.
it is a flood, and there
is no more sky.

the surf

Big Wave, Sheryl Massaro ©

in the water tunnel

in the dream,
the warm blue
of the curling wave.
light glinting
through perfect
calibration, again,
of the tubular.
sound holding breath,
exhale gathering.

in the dream,
the beauty of being,
of seeing the whirl
from within, twirling.

in this dream, a blanket
gently shaken over us,
or not gently, settling.
the tides, their waves.

surf

the waves held the moon
all night. the sun all day.
waves brought them ashore,
and took them away.
brought them, took them.
brought, took.

he remembered the surf,
how it left his feet
on what felt like pillars
of sand. he could see
the suds and bubbles
left behind as it ebbed.

too far away to see
and feel now, but
near enough to hear.
the pleasant shushing
drifted into his room,
rested with him on his bed,
and together they remembered
the pocked face of the moon
and the sun's bonfire,
both buoyed wherever
the oceans wander.

a hand of sunlight
touched his shoulder.
human, i want to be
with you. the hand
became a wing and he,
an old man napping,

turned to gold
in the daylight
borne by the surf
to his bed, and then
it brought the moon.

waking

i saw evil lifting
from earth in waves,
nearly invisible,
like heat. it was
a beautiful thing
to see it shimmer away,
to hear the land sigh
as if a terrible pain
had been relieved.
i saw evil radiate
from everywhere
on earth as if
i were in space,
witnessing.
what had been silence
became the soft sounds
of air and animals,
leaves and grasses
moving tentatively,
as if their breath
had been held
a long time. then
a brief rain came
and all was washed
and steaming.
quietly, happily
weeping. waking,
i wondered if we
would want to know
where the evil had gone,
or know what to do
if we found it.

rise & fall

in the kimberleys, australia,
the tides slosh through
gauntlets of inlets
to raise the bays 30 feet
or more, and then,
like a great herd of sheep
turning at the nip of a collie,
away they flee and spread
across the indian ocean.

in her time of want
she contemplates this daily glut,
wonders if, like birth canals,
the narrow waterways prepare
for the tidal onslaughts.

in this dried field of stalk
bones, she surveys the beiges
rippling in heat as far as eyes
can see. the wells are hollow,
the cisterns low, and she
is parched as well. beautiful
word, *cistern*, she thinks,
and *aqueduct*. graceful structures
built to hold and carry, tied
to ancient humans who had her thirst
and a land to heal.

her eyes narrow
as she strains to hear
the waters splashing
through the kimberleys
on the other side of earth.

the great wave

the ocean floor ruptures
an ember pops onto mulch
a paper cuts
there was one more step

was that a shudder in the earth
or in a dream that woke me?
moon and breeze ply the curtain,
tides shush.

we all smoked in the sixties,
a great era for introverts
who, at parties, could puff
on a patio and coolly
toss a butt into a pool,
onto flagstone, into mulch.
no thought but for how
to enter to the party again
without trembling.

contracts. one page, two pages,
a gazillion pages. property, cars,
grants. poems. one page, two pages,
ouch! three pages, drivel, fall asleep.

she was fit
but it was so late.
who falls *up* the stairs?
every bone on one side
hit the hickory floor.
she lay there and laughed
and could not get up.

the great wave off kanagawa,
hokusai's metaphor, perhaps,
for the gathering in
of countless goofs
until the mass wobbles
and the mass cascades.
a bone snaps,
a virus finds a papercut,
a smolder blazes in mulch,
a tsunami lifts from earth,
hovers in the strangeness
of air, and we await.

it isn't

pretend you are the first
human to hold an empty
conch. you wonder
if something tasty
is in there. shake it.
nothing.
hold it to your ear
to hear the creature
scratching. you hear
… ocean.
a low rumbling of waves
whorls its way through
the furled nacre, and then
the lick of flat tides
as they reach the shore.
there are gulls crying out,
whales slapping the surface.
some day, volleyball.
don't tell me it's blood surging
through my vascular network.
the ocean is in that shell.

intrusion

if i were a tide,
my foam would make
horizons, and sand
would be their skies.
if i were an ocean,
i would long for land
to come to rest in.
if i were land, i would be
a neutral country,
with porous borders.
i would be fertile,
my crops verdant
from sweet waters,
yet i would give a home
to a probing ocean.
if i gave a home to an ocean,
my sweetness would sour.
if i were sour, i would hold
another beauty, another peace,
and my flat, sour waters
would be filled with sky
and cloud and horizon.

estuaries

late afternoon,
the tidal waters
swell the marshes
and a scent travels
up the hill to us
almost like the tang
of oceans, yet evoking
a close, sheltered world
rather than horizons.

low terrains of salt
and fresh mingling,
the heavier, the lighter,
colder, warmer.
silvery barramundi in asia,
bald eagles in the americas,
oysters, mud crabs,
ancient horseshoes.
pickleweed, loosestrife.
adaptable survivors.
at night, coyotes.

a place where people come on purpose
to toss their disagreeing, puzzling words
onto the red mud and, face to face,
fit the strange angles into place.

coming together
is what
the aborigines believe
an estuary means.

bad water

this water has been
bad. very.
as bad as an evil queen
thinks she is.
but she is nothing
as bad as bad water.

the sun won't shine
through bad water.
in the dead realms
of algal fortresses,
no fishes go
corals long to leave
color goes to die.

you think the tides
are gravity playing
with the moon, but no.
they are the long breaths *in*
by the good water,
and the long exhales.
breathing, traveling,
tossing and turning,
living. good water.

we mourn the good
that falls to bad water.
motionless, littered
with centuries of us.
only a perfect storm
could clear it.

nude on blue

when do we begin? when cells foam
and bubble into being, haphazard thought
congealing in the tiny ocean of a womb?
when the heart starts and the spine grows taut

from rump to mind? or does our first dream
begin us, our first wonder, our first
wordless musing on the warm dark steam
of *where*, of forming all alone, immersed

in our pliant cave? or is it when we learn
out, yearning for a seventh wave to break
as when a last dream crests to bring
us *there*, plucking our toes from sand.

the pony swim

rose hip, cordgrass,
bayberry waver
in the salt marsh.
wild ponies listen to wind
in grasses, over water.
a low surf eddies and ebbs
just above their hooves.
manes and tails lift.

at slack tide,
the annual upheaval
to thin the herd begins.
saltwater cowboys
pick their ways through
scrub and loblolly pines
on the long island
and coax the ponies
from their peace,
to open channel,
to auction.

in a flurry, the foals
take to the water,
startling life that hides
in shells along the sand.
on the other shore wait
families longing to touch,
to tame, to love and to ride,
and a stall.

whales

not for the softness of deep waters
or their motions, tender and tingling
on the thin scalp of the heart.

not for this did they part from earth,
from mingling with grass and air and us.
it might have been god's moaning,

alone and floating in his rest,
that lured them from sands and jungles
to the waters and their pulse.

the spa

Great Egret, Sheryl Massaro ©

afloat

not interested
in plunging mysteries,
deeps, not interested
in clear critters thriving
where the sun can't reach,
in strange predators
prowling the wet channels
for flesh. just want to float
on top of an ocean,
ruminating, reading the sky,
discussing land with
the merpeople, its stability,
pitfalls. i nod off, at times,
and the merfolk kindly
keep me afloat. that
is how the helicopter
will find me as it searches
far and wide. thirsty,
but breathing. a single
pale human rocking gently
on a dark sea.
Then the boat will come,
and I'll be lifted from below
and from above.

the spa of the snow monkey

know water, know god
ice, pool, steam
god, child, spirit
one substance, but different

in daylight, rosy-faced
macaques slip through
the northern woods
and softly splash into
a thermal pool. mists
and vapors surround
them even as snow falls.
for a time, their eyes close
in unspeakable bliss.
the steam around them
thickens as if an emanation
of rapture. a newborn wakes
to suckle a fuchsia teat,
and the spell breaks.
many rest with forearms
crossed on the frozen banks,
as if catching up on gossip.
groomers pick.

so it goes in daylight.
in moonlight, the pool
and god sleep alone.

the damp

it's in the morning,
that bit of sweat
the darkness leaves
at its dawn death.
i bare my tongue
and lick the air quickly,
before the dampness
goes. it hides there, water,
in invisible things.
i feel it. i will find it
without the sunlight.
i'll listen for the whisper
of insect wings swarming
above a puddle.
i'll smell the musty pool
just under a low spot
of the dusty riverbed.
my soles will feel a heart
beat deep in the earth.
that is where the river lives
now, not with the sun
as many believe.

precipitation

i recall sitting in rain that fell
through sunlight, and driving in rain
that made roads disappear.
the first would be the *female rain*,
and the second the *male rain*,
as our native people say.
i recall impervious ice,
the hail-cracked windshields
of saskatchewan,
racing down snowy hills
on saucers, pungent woolens
burdened with burrs of snow.
i recall walking through early winter,
through the scent of woodsmoke,
through the delicate cold touch
of the first stars of snow
melting into skin.

in the house of waters

no dry place here,
no kindling to light
in all these rooms,
chairs and tables sodden,
afloat. a drawer drifts by,
its folded woolens cold,
smelling of snow
and red cheeks, cocoa.

they are not here,
those daily things
that keep the minutes
moving, weaving us
through our talismans
of home. the brush
against teeth, the stair creak,
the favorite cup touching
its spousal saucer.
the house's air, fresh
or full of coffee, wood fires,
mown grass, messages.

this air is heavy. each breath
from these rooms now is deep
and slow, as if wading through mercury,
as the waters wantonly touch floors,
walls, part the weighted curtains,
insinuate the contours of closets.
and in the baths, submerged tubs
anchor faint lusters of touch
from humans
who are not quite gone.

cicadas

cicadas flex their tymbals
in the high trees flanking
the lane. a quick rain,
and macadam steams.

hands probe for turnip,
carrot, radish, yam
deep in the red ground.
small rivers stutter
from brow to chin
through dried soil,
2-day stubble.

as if a stone is dropped
and the pond ripples,
one cicada chirps
and a chorale of dronings
lifts and sags, spreads far,
wide, and then returns,
an orbit ever roping in
the mates with this strange,
primitive song.

crusty lips glisten
with fresh water
from the old hose.
moisture blooms down
the throat, in the belly,
via every artery and vein
as if tissue were grass
turning green. the garden
and the gardener drink, rest.
the tymbals flex.

wet

we who are mostly water
have devised a wind turbine
that draws it drinkable
from the air

and we can purify water
with the physics of its own weight
and gravity to charge a bulb,
shedding a light that cleans

we compile books of silver-laced
paper for filtering the bacterium
that causes cholera

there is a cone that uses the sun
and evaporation to de-salinate

a billboard in peru yields 96 liters a day
from fog, and has a public faucet

there is a special straw
and a special ceramic

and $50,000 to those
who have other portable
purification solutions

but we have nothing
to keep water of any kind
from where we do not want it
if it is determined to come.

what is beautiful

why do we know that the grass
between our toes is soft or even green,
and why do we think green and soft
are nice things for grass to be,
and how do we know what *nice* is or that water
when liquid is delicate as it flows
through our fingers yet can break them
when chilled, and how is it that we know
the difference and know that knowing
makes a difference even though the knowing
is invisible and grass and sky and water
and you and I are not
... or are we? eventually we will be, and then
how will we know anything about anything
or will nothing matter or will everything matter
and with what will we determine this—
a sense, an organ, or with the hitherto
unrecognizable something with which i sense
the ongoing joys of the dead and gone,
with which i see, with something
other than sight, only beauty?

narcissus

we are asked to believe
a young man never knew
his beauty until he drank
from a still pool and,
like a bird in a mirror,
could not fathom
that this ravishing being
was himself.
or, *did* know it was
his own impossible beauty
and raged in frustration
of what he could not caress.
through his fingers it slipped,
his image splitting, spreading
to the far banks.

winter

the blue-black of sky
runs into me, carried
with the gust i breathe
in a gasp i cannot exhale.
how can they survive in this,
i think, the homeless?
the ones in tents
in the scruffland
at the edge of town,
how? do they turn in
as the dark comes,
zipped tight in a down bag?
mind closing, eyes blocking
random headlights, body
sinking into the kind of stasis
a youngster enters when
they fall through ice, yet survive.
but where are they,
until that breath comes?

freedom

countries come and go in the sky.
clouds turn in ribbons, birds veer in unison.

light casts its colors at will and flies away.
wonder, memory, perfection fill the mind's lake
behind an eye overwhelmed with horizons.

the eye of a man freed of a country.
a border *here* now is *there*,
a road now leads *from*, not *to*,
the stranger now is you,
and where you have left to go is *here.*

but here moves. it moves in questions,
in plans that make plans. it chills your skin,
ruffles your heart, rubs your eyes
as you watch the moon quiver
in every puddle as it moves
into all the sky's countries.

headache

the towel formed a tent around her head
as she bent over and inhaled steam
from the pot of simmering water.
persistent agony behind her eyes
began to ease, and breath found holes
in whatever bodily substance
had plugged her nostrils.
something deep in the back of her skull
began to separate, like glaciers thinning,
breaking into floes. the rest of her relaxed,
began to crave bed and sleep.
this discomfort was too much, she felt,
yet at least she could breathe by mouth.
the lungs were good.

she lifted her head and backed away
from the steam. right off, she was chilled
as her damp face woke to the winter room.
it would be like this for awhile:
the routine of heating the pot to a simmer,
then tenting to hoard the vapor
that slowly, magically cleared her head,
then backing into the world.

bag of waters

a dream baby came last night
in her *bag of waters* as they'd say
in the old days. she took 8 minutes,
wincing and blinking at the light
and many faces, and then
i held her toes
and cupped her feet
and our eyes met,
our eyes held,
and we smiled
at our tacit bond
in this strange world.
and then i woke up,
amazed that there
had been no pain.

first bath

he rested in the bend of her arm
as she cupped the soapy water
and drizzled it down his miniature torso,
sudsed up his soft, bald head,
fondled each toe.

he looked into her as if he were elsewhere,
as if this wasn’t real. he was afloat and,
for a moment, still was pending in wet,
muffled dark. and then a warmed towel
wrapped this skin that now could feel.
his eyes found light and color. everywhere.

ablutions

in the backyard with its creek
and big trees, i was caught
in ecstatic play by an *aha*,
a sudden adult awareness
in my very young mind
that i was astonishingly happy,
one of many fleshly giggles
incarnate who were meant
to play and imagine and spin
lightness around the grownups
with our little voices. in return,
fragrant wood lit our fireplaces,
our kitchens were close and warm,
sofas big and soft for nestling.
and the days ended with a splash
in the tub, the ritual ablutions,
when suds rinsed away
everything but play.

grapes

in the museum's
old food room
on a sweltering day,
a cluster of reds a century old
hangs from a gold string
against a subtle backdrop
in an artist's studio.
behind our polite interest,
we are hot, thirsty, desperate
to pluck a cold, sweet grape.

but the 400-year old,
blushing anjou over there
looks even juicier.
so easy to feel our teeth
sinking into its pale flesh,
nectar gathering,
dripping off our chins.

and a melon, sliced
open in the 1400s—
our frantic fingers
yearn to fling its pulp
and seeds to the marble floor,
leaving behind for us
the near-liquid fruit-meat
of old, fertile europe.

but there is the guard,
and he is watching.
unquenched, we leave
the masterpieces intact,
the old food untouched.

we find the sweltering outside
has brought storms,
gushers, and i marvel
at how water, rain,
for months enters a blossom
and then its growing fruit
so that, eventually,
even in drought
we can drink.

the water tasting

she knelt at one end
of the long table
so that only one side
of the first bottle was visible,
and then she shifted
to the left, in increments,
so that each next bottle
down the line
slowly came into view,
prisms at their feet
from the warm sun
behind them.

so went her ritual
at every tasting
to keep her from taking
these waters for granted.
so many, from so many places,
each a magical fluid.

she would not be today's
only water sommelier.
there always were a few,
each bearing a keen eye,
the nose of a bloodhound,
discerning tastebuds,
an exquisite thirst.

they could taste rock
earth minerals textures
sweetness saltiness
in waters from everywhere.
the taste of the terroir

of each selection
filtered through mountains,
siphoned from deep layers
of freshwater ice age melt
that sank and stayed
on the ocean floor,
the thaws of glaciers,
the cores of icebergs,
groundwaters, rain.
bubbly, still.

to perch on this table,
a water must be raw,
untouched, unpurified,
thousands of years old.
it must be respected
by the locals,
who are its protectors,
drink it daily,
claim healing or miracles
or blue zone lifespans
for generations.

hype. a miracle healing,
the romans bathed here,
from a secret sacred
polynesian spring,
the purest water from
the heart of ancient ice
that is no more. she knew

her ribbon would go
to the crisp german,
the one who did the least
to the magic of all waters.

stars

the stars always are visible,
even at noon,
from the bottom of a well.

there, when you raise your eyes
to the circle of light at the end
of the damp stone tunnel.

there when you stare into
the puddle at your feet.

there when the stone and sky
are the same ink.

Sheryl Massaro is an oil painter, poet, and photographer based in Frederick, MD. She holds an MFA in Creative Writing/Poetry from The American University and studied with several key poets, including Allen Ginsberg, Stanley Kunitz, W.S. Merwin, et al. Her other books of poetry include *Rilke's Duino Elegies—An Interpretive Translation,* and *The Hood of Evening* and *A Generation,* collections of her poems from a 30-year period.

Massaro's visual art and poetry, though often based on the recognizable, share a deeper, "off to the side" look at life than the purely representational. In each of these arts, she taps into and conveys life's undertow—the unspoken, unseen energy that brings close and binds artists and their readers or viewers.

Massaro's visual art is carried by DISTRICT Arts Gallery and the FAC/Hurwitz Gallery in Frederick, MD. For information on her books and art, please visit sherylmassaro.com.